BREAKING GENERATIONAL CURSES

A Guide to Overcoming Generational Curses and Embracing a Future of Blessings.

RACHEL TUGUTU

Copyright © 2024 Rachel Tugutu

All rights reserved.

ISBN: 9783235958926

DEDICATION

"Christ hath redeemed us from the curse of the law, being made a curse for us: for it is written, Cursed is every one that hangeth on a tree: That the blessing of Abraham might come on the Gentiles through Jesus Christ; that we might receive the promise of the Spirit through faith."

— Galatians 3:13-14 King James Version (KJV)

Table of Contents

Introduction: The Weight of Generational Curses

Chapter 1: Understanding Generational Curses
- Defining Generational Curses
- Biblical Foundations and Examples

Chapter 2: The Cycle of Patterns: Recognizing Your Family's History
- Identifying Relational Dynamics
- Emotional and Spiritual Roots of Curses

- ★ Biblical Way to Recognize the Cycle of Patterns

Chapter 3: Faith as a Foundation: The Power of Belief

- ★ Embracing Faith in God
- ★ The Role of Spiritual Trust and Obedience
- ★ Biblical Principals and Guidelines

Chapter 4: Power in Your Authority: Claiming Your Identity in Christ

- ★ Understanding Your Inheritance
- ★ Practical Steps to Embrace Your Authority

- ★ The Biblical way to claim your authority in Christ

Chapter 5: Breaking Free: Steps to Overcome Curses
- ★ Acknowledgment and Confession
- ★ Forgiveness as a Key to Healing
- ★ Practical Exercises for Breaking Chains with Biblical support

Chapter 6: Rewriting Your Story: Creating a New Legacy
- ★ Setting New Patterns for Future Generations

- ★ Declaring Generational Blessings

Chapter 7: Cultivating a Mindset of Abundance
- ★ Shifting from Scarcity to Abundance
- ★ Scriptural Insights and Daily Affirmations

Chapter 8: The Importance of Community
- ★ Building Support Systems
- ★ The Role of Mentorship and Accountability

Closing: A Journey of Hope and Transformation

Appendix: Resources for Further Study

Lists of Bible Verses to Help You Meditate to Break Generational Curses

Acknowledgment

INTRODUCTION

The Weight of Generational Curses

Throughout our lives, we frequently find ourselves entangled in patterns that appear to repeat—cycles of pain, hardship, and confusion that can leave us feeling trapped. At first glance, these patterns might seem coincidental, mere happenstance in the grand tapestry of our experiences. However, what if these recurring issues are not random at all? What if they are the manifestation of generational curses—spiritual burdens that have been passed down through our family lineage, embedded in our very existence?

In our exploration titled "Breaking the Chains," we will embark on a profound journey to uncover and understand these invisible chains that bind us. This journey is not merely about identifying the issues; it's about delving deeply into the roots of these generational patterns, examining their origins, and gaining insight into how they have influenced our lives.

We will examine the profound and lasting effects of unresolved past traumas, persistent fears that linger in our subconscious, and recurring failures that can create a persistent sense of defeat and despair. These elements often shape our perceptions, behaviors, and choices, continuing to impact our lives unless we confront and address them head-on.

Through this exploration, we aim to equip you with practical tools and strategies designed to help break free from these debilitating cycles. Together, we will navigate the complexities of our familial histories and empower ourselves to re-write our own narratives. By understanding these forces at play, we can begin the transformative process of healing and liberation, reclaiming our lives from the shadows of the past and stepping boldly into a future defined by freedom and possibility.

CHAPTER 1

Understanding Generational Curses

Defining Generational Curses

Generational curses are often described as the patterns of sin, dysfunction, and adverse circumstances that span multiple generations within a family line. These patterns may manifest in various ways, including addiction, behavioral issues, unhealthy relationships, or financial difficulties. The concept suggests that familial sins and negative experiences are not just isolated incidents;

instead, they are inherited by descendants, who may find themselves repeating the same damaging patterns.

The term "curse" can conjure up images of dark magic or witchcraft, but in this context, it refers to the consequences of forsaken principles and choices made by previous generations. When a family has not addressed its internal strife, unresolved trauma, or sin, these elements can create a cycle that becomes increasingly difficult to break.

Each generation inherits not only the legacies of their ancestors' values, beliefs, and lessons but also their struggles and mistakes. From a psychological standpoint, this can be understood through concepts like transgenerational trauma or historical trauma, which indicate that emotional pain can travel through familial lines, affecting individuals who are unaware of their roots.

Understanding generational curses allows individuals to look beyond mere behavior and to explore the underlying causes of persistent issues. It provides a framework for understanding how past traumas, choices, and relational patterns can influence current behavior and choices.

Biblical Foundations and Examples

The Bible provides a theological backdrop for understanding generational curses, grounding the concept in spiritual terms. At its core, the idea suggests a divine framework of justice where choices have consequences that resonate through the fabric of familial legacy.

Old Testament Perspective

In the Old Testament, a key reference point is found in Exodus 20:5-6, where God addresses Moses regarding idolatry: "You shall not bow down to them or serve them; for I, the Lord your God, am a jealous God, visiting the iniquity of the fathers upon the children to the third and fourth generation of those who hate Me, but showing mercy to thousands, to those who love Me and keep My commandments." This passage illustrates a profound truth: the actions of the fathers can influence the lives of their children and even their grandchildren.

Other passages, such as Deuteronomy 5:9-10 and Numbers 14:18, reinforce this notion, indicating that the consequences of sin can echo through generations. Additionally, the story of King David exemplifies how sin may lead to generational ramifications—his adultery with Bathsheba resulted in turmoil within his family, as illustrated by the tragic fates of his children.

New Testament Perspective

In the New Testament, while the focus shifts toward personal accountability and grace, the concept of generational curses can still find relevance. The teachings of Christ emphasize the need for repentance and transformation, and through His sacrifice, believers are offered the opportunity to break free from the chains of their ancestry.

Galatians 3:13-14 affirms that "Christ has redeemed us from the curse of the law, having become a curse for us." This means that believers can break ties with generational strongholds through faith in Jesus. The promise of renewal and rebirth provides hope, demonstrating that although individuals may inherit certain tendencies or patterns from their families, they are not condemned to repeat them.

Examples of Generational Curses in Scripture

1. **The House of Jeroboam**: Jeroboam, the first king of the northern kingdom of

Israel, established idolatry that tainted his lineage. As a result, God foretold that his house would be cut off (1 Kings 14:10), demonstrating the lasting repercussions of his sinful actions.

2. **The Lineage of Abraham**: The

patriarch Abraham's decision to lie about Sarah being his sister (Genesis 20) created a legacy of deceit. Later, we see his grandson Jacob deceiving his father Isaac (Genesis 27), showing that the thread of dishonesty wove its way through the family.

3. **Manasseh**: King Manasseh of Judah exemplifies a generational curse through his actions. His reign was marked by idolatry, which led to Israel's corruption (2 Kings 21), and though he repented towards the end of his life, the

damage to his lineage and nation persisted.

In conclusion, gaining a deeper understanding of generational curses through a biblical perspective offers profound insights into the complexities of the human experience. This exploration of inherent patterns and behavioral tendencies that are often passed down through family lines reveals not only the spiritual ramifications but also the emotional and psychological effects on subsequent generations.

Recognizing the influence of past generations on our present circumstances is a pivotal first step towards breaking free from the chains that may hold future generations captive. By practicing mindfulness and bringing attention to these familial patterns, individuals can begin to identify recurring cycles of behavior that may not serve them well. This awareness paves the way for seeking forgiveness—both from oneself and from others—for any harm inflicted, whether intentional or unintentional, by previous generations.

Moreover, embracing a transformative faith can serve as a powerful catalyst for change. This faith encourages individuals to reimagine their narratives, allowing them to reclaim their identities free from the weight of ancestral burdens. As we embark on this enlightening journey, delving into the various facets of generational curses, we will gradually uncover layers of understanding that illuminate paths toward freedom.

Healing often comes through the process of confronting these deep-seated issues, and as each layer is peeled back, the opportunity for generational blessings emerges. By actively engaging in this process of healing and restoration, we can cultivate new legacies characterized by strength, resilience, and grace that positively impact not only ourselves but also those who come after us. Ultimately, this journey leads to the realization of a brighter future, unfettered

by the past.

CHAPTER 2

The Cycle of Patterns: Recognizing Your Family's History

The Cycle of Patterns Identifying Relational Dynamics

As we journey deeper into understanding the

cycles of our family history, we must first turn our gaze inward, examining the intricate web of relational dynamics that shape our experiences and behaviors. Just as a spider weaves its web with meticulous precision, so too do families weave patterns of interaction that can endure for generations. These dynamics are often subtle, underlying emotional scripts that dictate how we relate to one another, love one another, and even how we perceive ourselves.

To identify these patterns, we must undertake a careful analysis of our family tree. Start by asking essential questions:

1. **Communication Styles**: How did your family members communicate? Were emotions freely expressed, or was there a strict code of silence? Did arguments escalate quickly, or was a passive-aggressive approach more common?

Understanding how your family interacted can shed light on your own communication style.

2. **Roles Within the Family**: Every family has roles that evolve over time. Who was the peacemaker, the rebel, the nurturer? Did

certain members take on responsibilities that were not theirs to bear? Noticing these roles can reveal underlying patterns of behavior that may be at play in your life today.

3. **Conflict Resolution**: How did your family handle conflict? Did

they confront issues head-on, or did they sweep them under the rug? The way conflict is resolved in our families can create lasting impressions, influencing how we manage disagreements in our own relationships.

4. **Support Systems**: Examining the support structures within your family is crucial. Were there strong bonds of support, or did members operate in isolation? The level of support we experienced as children often dictates what we

expect—or fear—from others in adulthood.

By delving into these relational dynamics, we can begin to recognize patterns not only in how we interact with family members but also in how we engage with friends, partners, and colleagues. This recognition is a vital step in breaking free from negative cycles and forging healthier connections.

Emotional and Spiritual Roots of Curses

Having identified the relational dynamics within our families, we must now confront a more challenging aspect of our history: the emotional and spiritual roots of curses. These 'curses' manifest as repeating cycles of dysfunction, trauma, and pain that echo through generations, often rooted in unresolved issues passed down from our ancestors.

1. **Understanding Family Curses**: Family curses often arise from deep emotional wounds—grief, anger, betrayal—that remain unhealed.

These injuries bind us to the past, creating legacies of pain and addiction, loneliness, or failure. They can be as visible as a pattern of premature death or as insidious as chronic tension in relationships. Recognizing these patterns is the first step toward healing.

2. **The Role of Trauma**: Historical traumas experienced by our families—war, displacement, loss—can ripple through generations, affecting emotional health and relationships. Trauma can distort the lens through which we view

the world, leading to anxiety and fear that inhibit our ability to connect with others meaningfully.

3. **Spiritual Connections**: Many cultures believe that unresolved issues can leave spiritual imprints, tying us to the burdens of our

forebears. Rituals, ancestral healing practices, and acts of forgiveness can serve as powerful tools in breaking these ties. By engaging in these traditions, we honor our lineage while liberating ourselves from its unbroken grasp.

4. **Breaking the Cycle**: The most crucial aspect of addressing these emotional and spiritual roots is the commitment to break the cycle. This can be achieved through therapy, spiritual practices, or simply through conscious awareness and active effort. Recognizing that

we have the power to change our narrative is empowering, as it positions us not just as victims of past circumstances but as active agents of change.

Conclusion

As we weave together the threads of relational dynamics and the emotional and spiritual roots of curses, we begin to see how our families shape us and how we, in turn, shape our legacies. Understanding these cycles is the first step toward healing and transformation.

****

In the labyrinth of our lives, we often find ourselves walking paths forged by those who came before us. These paths, marked by familial relationships, emotional legacies, and spiritual influences, create a cyclical pattern that shapes our identity and behaviors. This chapter invites you to step back and examine these patterns, encouraging an exploration into the relational dynamics that influence our lives. Understanding these cycles can illuminate the emotional and spiritual roots of curses—those burdens we carry from our past—and guide us toward a biblical way of recognizing and breaking free from them.

Identifying Relational Dynamics

Relational dynamics within families often reflect deeply ingrained patterns of behavior. These may manifest as repetitive conflicts, unspoken expectations, or ingrained roles that family members unconsciously fulfill. Acknowledging these dynamics is the first step in understanding their impact.

Start by creating a family tree, not just with names and dates, but with the relational flows — identifying who got along, who didn't, and the significant events that are part of your family lore. This exercise is akin to fingerprinting your family history. Can you see a tendency towards conflict in one branch of the family tree? Notice how certain emotional responses seem to echo through generations?

A critical aspect of relational dynamics is communication. Examine your family's communication style. Was it open and nurturing, or closed and punitive? Reflect on how these patterns shape your interactions. Do you find yourself repeating certain phrases or behaviors that echo your parents or grandparents? As you identify these dynamics, allow yourself to feel the weight and significance of their presence in your life.

Emotional and Spiritual Roots of Curses

As we delve into the emotional aspects of familial history, we must confront the notion of "curses," not in the superstitious sense, but as patterns of behavior that can feel imprisoning. These may include cycles of addiction, abuse, mental health struggles, or poverty that appear intertwined with family genetics or histories. The burdens we inherit can sometimes feel like a curse, restricting our ability to thrive.

From an emotional standpoint, these patterns often carry trauma. Consider how unresolved issues or unhealed wounds can reverberate through generations. For example, a family that suffered loss may have developed an aversion to attachment, leading future generations to struggle with commitment or intimacy.

Spiritually, many traditions, including biblical teachings, speak of generational sins and blessings (Exodus 20:5-6). These teachings remind us that our actions can carry implications beyond our lifetimes. Reflect on this: what are the unhealed emotional wounds within your family? Have they been addressed, or do they linger, passed down like heirlooms? Understanding the emotional and spiritual roots of these patterns can provide clarity on how to navigate and potentially break free from them.

Biblical Way to Recognize the Cycle of Patterns

The Bible offers a framework for recognizing and addressing these cycles. Scriptures like 2 Corinthians 5:17 remind us that in Christ, we are new creations; the old has passed away. This promise invites us to confront our past with hope, understanding that we are not bound to repeat the mistakes of our forebears.

Engage with biblical narratives that illustrate family patterns. Consider the story of Joseph, who, despite being sold into slavery by his brothers, rose to greatness and reconciled with his family, breaking the cycle of jealousy and betrayal within his lineage. Reflect on the transformative grace that allowed him to forgive and redefine his family's future.

In your own journey, prayer and meditation can be powerful tools. Ask God to reveal the patterns in your family history that need healing. Meditate on passages that speak of redemption and restoration, allowing these truths to root deeply in your heart.

Journaling is another effective method for recognizing these cycles. Write down what you discover about your family dynamics, emotional burdens, and spiritual influences. Reflect on how they align or conflict with your own pursuits and beliefs.

Conclusion

As we conclude this chapter, remember that recognizing the cycle of patterns in your family's history is not about placing blame but rather understanding the intricate web of relationships and legacies that have shaped you. Embrace the opportunity not just to identify these influences but also to transform them.

By acknowledging the past, you empower yourself to forge a new legacy, one that reflects healing, growth, and divine promise. You possess the ability to break the cycles of hurt and fear, releasing future generations into the freedom and purpose that God designed for each of us. Step forward with courage, for the journey of discovery and healing begins with you.

In the following chapters, we will delve deeper into specific techniques and practices for recognizing and breaking these patterns, helping us to rewrite the stories of our ancestors and forge connections grounded in love, understanding, and acceptance. In doing so, we can move beyond the cycles of the past and create a future filled with possibility and hope.

CHAPTER 3

Faith as a Foundation: The Power of Belief

In a world often shrouded in uncertainty, where chaos seems to reign and doubt creeps into our hearts, the foundational tenet of faith stands resiliently as an unwavering anchor. Faith, particularly faith in God, is more than a mere abstract concept; it is a powerful force that shapes our lives, guiding us through trials, illuminating our paths, and shaping our destinies. In this chapter, we will delve into the transformative power of belief, explore the role of spiritual trust and obedience, and examine biblical principles and guidelines that fortify our faith.

Embracing Faith in God

The journey of faith begins with a conscious decision to embrace belief. It is an act of the will—a resolute choice to trust in a higher purpose and a divine plan. The Bible teaches us that faith is not merely the absence of doubt but an active commitment to believe despite uncertainties (Hebrews 11:1). Consider the story of Abraham, who is often hailed as the father of faith. He embarked on a journey to an unknown land, leaving behind all that was familiar because he chose to trust in God's promise (Genesis 12:1-4). This act of faith embodies the essence of bravely stepping into the unknown, driven by the conviction that God's plan is better than our own.

In our own lives, we are often called to take similar leaps of faith. Whether it is embarking on a new career, exiting unhealthy relationships, or seeking spiritual growth, we must learn to let go of our fears and uncertainties. Embracing faith in God means surrendering our limited understanding to the infinite wisdom of the Divine. It is about recognizing that we are part of a much larger narrative, one that we cannot always comprehend but can trust nonetheless.

The Role of Spiritual Trust and Obedience

Faith is not a passive state; it is a dynamic practice that requires ongoing trust and obedience. When we place our faith in God, we must also be willing to align our lives with His teachings. Spiritual trust involves believing wholeheartedly in God's promises and His character. It is the confidence that He is good, loving, and just and that He desires what is best for us.

Obedience follows trust like a shadow follows a body. When we truly believe in God's goodness, we feel compelled to act by His will. This idea is beautifully illustrated in the life of Moses, who trusted God's call to lead the Israelites out of Egypt. Despite his initial fears and feelings of inadequacy, Moses obeyed God's command and became a vessel of miraculous liberation (Exodus 3-14).

Obedience is not a call to blind adherence but an invitation to step into a deeper relationship with God. It is an act of faith that reflects our trust in His wisdom. As we learn to obey, our faith grows stronger, allowing us to endure challenges and remain steadfast in the face of adversity.

Biblical Principles and Guidelines

The Bible is rich with principles and guidelines that offer us insights into the nature of faith and its application in our lives. Here are some essential biblical teachings that underscore the importance of faith as a foundation:

1. **Faith is a Gift**: Ephesians 2:8-9 teaches us that faith is a gift from God, not something we can earn. This understanding fosters humility and gratitude

as we recognize that our ability to believe stems from divine grace.

2. **Faith Involves Action**: James 2:17 clearly states that faith without action is dead. True faith manifests itself through our deeds and intentions. When we believe, our actions

should reflect our beliefs, showing the world the impact that faith has on our lives.

3. **Faith Overcomes Fear**: Throughout scripture, we are reminded to "fear not." Isaiah 41:10 encourages us with the assurance that God is with us. Trusting in His

presence allows us to rise above fear and embrace confidence as we navigate life's uncertainties.

4. **Community of Believers**: Hebrews 10:24-25 highlights the importance of gathering together in faith. The support and

encouragement of a faith community strengthen our journeys and remind us that we are not alone in our struggles.

5. **Perseverance in Faith**: James 1:2-4 teaches us that trials produce perseverance, which perfects our faith.

> Challenges are growth opportunities, refining us and drawing us closer to God.

As we meditate on these principles, we must remember that faith is not simply a response to good times but a commitment to trust in every season of life. In a world where change is the only constant, let us hold fast to the foundation of our belief.

Conclusion

Faith serves as a foundation that supports us through life's tumultuous seas. It invites us to embark on a journey of trust and obedience, shaping our lives in alignment with God's divine will. As we embrace faith in God, lean into spiritual trust, and uphold biblical principles, we transform not only our lives but also the lives of those around us. In doing so, we become beacons of light, illuminating the path for others and revealing the profound beauty of a life founded on unwavering belief. As we conclude this chapter, let us be inspired to deepen our faith, allowing it to be the bedrock upon which we build our lives, guiding us closer to our Creator in every step we take.

CHAPTER 4

Power in Your Authority: Claiming Your Identity in Christ

Understanding Your Inheritance

As believers, we often talk about our relationship with

Christ, but how often do we fully grasp the depth of what that relationship entails? The moment we accept Jesus Christ as our Lord and Savior, we are not merely adding another belief to our lives; we are entering into an entirely new identity and inheritance.

The Bible tells us in Ephesians 1:3 that we are blessed with every spiritual blessing in the heavenly places in Christ. This inheritance is not a distant reality but a present one, sculpted from the love of God and the sacrifice of His Son. Our identity in Christ transforms us; we are no longer defined by our past mistakes, by labels placed upon us by society, or by our current circumstances.

Instead, we are new creations (2 Corinthians 5:17), citizens of a heavenly kingdom, heirs to God's promises, and bearers of His authority here on earth.

This inheritance means more than just a future hope; it empowers us to live victoriously in the present. Understanding our identity in Christ allows us to step into the authority He gave us—not to wield power over others but to become instruments of His love, grace, and truth.

Practical Steps to Embrace Your Authority

Knowing that you have authority in Christ is only the beginning; you must actively embrace and exercise that authority in your daily life.

Here are some practical steps to help you do just that:

1. Study the Word of God:

- Immerse yourself in Scripture to understand the promises of God and your identity in Christ. Passages like Romans 8:17, Galatians 3:26-29, and Ephesians 2:19 are vital in reinforcing your identity as a child of God and an heir to His kingdom.

2. Prayer and Application:

- Engage in constant dialogue with God. Pray for wisdom and revelation regarding your identity and authority. Don't just pray; act on what you learn. For instance, if you feel called to counsel others, don't wait for someone to invite you to do it—start offering your support right away.

3. Declare and Confess:

- The tongue holds the power of life and death (Proverbs 18:21). Start speaking declarations over your life and the lives of those around you based on Scripture. For example, say, "I am a child of God," or "I have the authority to overcome every challenge through Christ who strengthens me."

4. Surround Yourself with Believers:

- Fellowship with like-minded believers who encourage you in your walk with Christ. Being in a community reinforces your identity and helps you to grow in authority as you support one another.

5. Step Into Opportunities:

- Look for opportunities to serve, lead, or share your faith. Each time you take a step of faith, you exercise the authority given to you by Christ. Remember, your authority is not just for yourself but is meant to extend to those around you.

The Biblical Way to Claim Your Authority in Christ

Claiming your authority in Christ must always align with the truth of God's Word. Here's how you can do that biblically:

1. Receive Your Identity:

- Accept that you are who God says you are. Free yourself from the past and societal labels. In

Christ, you are chosen, called, and cherished.

2. Know the Source of Your Authority:

- Understand that your authority comes from Jesus, not from your abilities or achievements. In Matthew 28:18, Jesus declared, "All authority in heaven and on earth has been given to me." As His followers, we tap into that divine authority.

3. Action Through Faith:

- In James 2:26, we learn that faith without works is dead. When you believe in your identity and authority, put it into action. Don't wait for feelings; obey God and act on His Word.

4. Use Your Authority Wisely:

- The authority given to you is not for self-gain or dominance over others; it is the power to serve, love, and lead others to Christ. Use your authority to bring healing, hope, and truth to a world in need.

5. Persist in the Battle:

- Spiritual authority comes with opposition. Ephesians 6:12 reminds us that we wrestle not against flesh and blood, but against spiritual forces. Stand firm in your authority through prayer, worship, and reliance on God's Word.

As you embrace your identity in Christ and acknowledge the authority you have been given, remember that it is a journey of faith. Continue to grow in understanding, steadfastly declare who you are, and actively participate in God's kingdom work. Your authority is powerful, not because of you, but because of Him who lives within you. Live boldly, for you are a child of the King!

CHAPTER 5

Breaking Free: Steps to Overcome Curses

Introduction

In every culture and belief system, the notion of curses—be they generational, spiritual, or self-imposed—has persisted throughout history. These curses can manifest as negative thought patterns, toxic relationships, or cyclical failures that hinder our progress and happiness. However, there's a path to liberation that begins with understanding and actively pursuing freedom through acknowledgment, forgiveness, and practical steps founded upon biblical principles.

Acknowledgment and Confession

The first step in breaking free from any curse is acknowledgment. Denial can be a powerful barrier, but facing the reality of our struggles is crucial for healing. This might involve a personal inventory, where we reflect on our lives, identifying patterns that suggest a curse might be in play.

- **Self-Reflection Exercise**: Take time to journal your thoughts and experiences. Ask yourself the following questions:
  - Do I notice repeated

negative patterns in my life?

- Are there unresolved issues or traumas affecting my well-being?
- What family dynamics or expectations have I internalized that

may be holding me back?

Once you've acknowledged these patterns, the next step is confession. Confessing not only to God but also to trusted friends or mentors can bring about a release of shame and guilt. James 5:16 (NIV) states, "Therefore confess your sins to each other and pray for each other so that you may be healed." Confession is not just about admitting wrongs; it's about opening a door to the healing process.

- **Confession Prayer**: Take some time in prayer, confessing your struggles to God. Ask for His guidance and strength to overcome the burdens you have been carrying. Use this moment to express gratitude for His grace.

Forgiveness as a Key to Healing

Forgiveness is often the most challenging step, yet it is essential for breaking the chains that bind us. Holding onto resentment can perpetuate a cycle of negativity, tying us to the very curses we long to escape. Jesus teaches us the importance of forgiveness, reminding us in Matthew 6:14-15 (NIV), "For if you forgive other people when they sin against you, your heavenly Father will also forgive you. But if you do not forgive others their sins, your Father will not forgive your sins."

- **Forgiveness Exercise**: Identify individuals or situations you need to forgive, including yourself. Write their names down on a piece of paper. Take a moment to pray over this list and ask God for the strength to forgive. When ready, physically tear the paper or set it ablaze as a symbol of releasing the past.

Practical Exercises for Breaking Chains with Biblical Support

1. **Scripture Memorization:**

Romans 12:2 (NIV) says, "Do not conform to the pattern of this world, but be transformed by the renewing of your mind." To transform your mindset, choose a verse that speaks to overcoming curses or personal struggles. Write it out and place it where you can see it daily. Repeating this verse will help anchor your thoughts in the truth of God's promises.

2. **Prayer and Fasting**: Engage in a period of prayer and fasting, focusing specifically on breaking curses and seeking God's intervention. Set aside dedicated time to pray, seeking divine assistance to break free from the burdens you

are experiencing. Matthew 17:21 (NIV) reminds us, "But this kind does not go out except by prayer and fasting."

3. **Accountability Partner**: It's essential to identify someone you trust deeply, someone who understands your

goals and aspirations, to serve as your accountability partner. This individual can play a crucial role in your journey, providing not only encouragement and motivation, but also invaluable support as you navigate the often complex emotional landscape of breaking free from challenges. An accountability partner serves as a reliable sounding board—offering advice, sharing experiences, and lending a listening ear when you're feeling overwhelmed or discouraged.

The connection you establish can help foster mutual growth, as both partners share their progress and setbacks. It's important to have regular check-ins, whether through weekly meetings, phone calls, or messages, to discuss milestones and reflect on what methods are working or where adjustments might be needed. As highlighted in Ecclesiastes 4:9-10 (NIV), "Two are better than one, because they have a good return for their labor: If either of them falls down, one can help the other up." This scripture underscores the importance of companionship and collaboration in overcoming difficulties, showing that supporting one another enhances the overall journey towards personal growth and success.

Conclusion

Breaking free from the burdens of curses is rarely an instantaneous occurrence; rather, it unfolds as a profound journey marked by conscious choices, unwavering commitment, and deep-rooted faith. The first step in this transformative process involves acknowledging and confessing the presence of the curse in one's life. This act of recognition is crucial, as it opens the door to healing and liberation.

Once you've named the curse, the next significant step is to embrace the transformative power of forgiveness. This includes not only forgiving others who may have caused harm but also allowing yourself to be forgiven, highlighting the importance of self-compassion in this journey.

To further facilitate this journey, actively engaging in practical exercises that are grounded in scripture is essential. These exercises might include daily prayer, meditation on specific biblical verses, or participating in supportive community groups that share similar goals of healing. Each of these practices acts as a tool to help shatter the chains that have kept you in bondage.

It's important to remember that every step taken in faith—regardless of its size—brings you closer to the abundant life that God has designed for you.

As you embark on this courageous journey towards freedom, it's vital to place your trust in His promises. Cling tightly to the truth of His Word, for it serves as your foundation and guide through the complexities of this path. This process may take time, but with patience and perseverance, you can ultimately experience the liberation and fullness of life that God intends for you.

CHAPTER 6

Rewriting Your Story: Creating a New Legacy

Setting New Patterns for Future Generations

Life often feels like a series of stories, woven together by the threads of our experiences, beliefs, and choices. As we navigate through the winding roads of existence, we begin to realize that we are not only the protagonists of our own narratives but also the authors who hold the pen of our future. This chapter focuses on the transformative act of rewriting your story—an act not just for your own benefit, but for the generations that will follow.

To create a new legacy, one must first acknowledge the existing narratives—both the empowering tales and the limiting ones that have been handed down. These stories often dictate how we view ourselves and the world. They shape our behaviors, decisions, and even our dreams. However, understanding that stories can be rewritten opens the door to endless possibilities. By consciously choosing to change the narrative, we create new patterns that future generations will inherit.

The Power of Self-Reflection

The journey of rewriting your story begins with self-reflection. Take a moment to consider the narratives that have influenced your life. What beliefs have you held about success, failure, love, and fear? How have these beliefs shaped your actions? Write them down as a way of acknowledging their presence in your life.

Next, envision the life you wish to create—not just for

yourself, but for your children, grandchildren, and beyond. What new patterns would you like to establish? These might include:

1. **Emotional Resilience**: Instead of viewing failure as a brutal end, model the idea that it's a stepping stone to growth. Teach your children to embrace

challenges as opportunities to learn.

2. **Open Communication**: Encourage transparency in your family. Create an environment where feelings and thoughts can be shared freely, breaking the cycle of

silence or misunderstanding.

3. **Value of Education and Curiosity**: Foster a love for learning by making it a shared family value. Help future generations see knowledge as a lifelong pursuit, not just a path to a degree.

4. **Financial Literacy**: Teach the principles of responsible financial management so that subsequent generations understand the importance of saving, investing, and giving back.
5. **Gratitude and Giving**: Instill the practice of

gratitude and the habit of giving back to the community, creating a legacy of compassion and responsibility.

Declaring Generational Blessings

Once you're clear on the new story you wish to write, the next step is to declare generational blessings. This is an act of intention, a way to affirm the legacy you are crafting. A blessing is not just a wish; it's a commitment to nurture and protect the values, beliefs, and practices that will enhance the lives of your descendants.

Conduct a family gathering to declare these blessings. This can be a formal event or a simple family dinner where everyone can participate. Use this occasion to articulate the new stories you are embracing, sharing your vision for the future. For instance:

- "May our family always value resilience, learning from setbacks as opportunities for growth."

- "May we communicate openly and honestly, knowing that love and understanding are the foundations of our relationships."
- "May we cherish the joy of giving back, understanding that our true wealth lies in the impact we have on others."

Each declaration is a seed planted into the fertile ground of your family's legacy. As you share these blessings, encourage your family to share their own aspirations, building a collective tapestry of hope and purpose.

Practical Steps for Legacy Building

As you embark on this transformative journey of writing your new legacy, consider these practical steps:

1. **Create a Family Vision Board**: Gather around, cut out images and words that represent your shared dreams and intentions. Display this vision board prominently in your

home as a daily reminder of your collective aspirations.

2. **Document Your Family History**: Create a family book that details your journey, including stories of triumph, lessons learned, and the new patterns you aim to

establish. This will serve as a reference, a reminder, and a source of inspiration for generations to come.

3. **Establish Family Traditions**: Create rituals that align with your new narrative. This could involve annual family retreats,

volunteer days, or even simple sharing of stories over meals. Traditions help to solidify the patterns you wish to set.

4. **Mentor Your Children**: Take time to engage individually with your children—teach them the values you cherish. Share lessons learned

from your life experiences so they might navigate their journeys with wisdom.

5. **Practice Forgiveness**: Understand that rewriting your story may involve letting go of past grievances. Model forgiveness within your family, reinforcing the

idea that it's never too late to alter course and build stronger, healthier relationships.

6. **Be a Living Example**: Finally, embody the change you wish to see. Your actions will speak louder than words, and your dedication to creating a new legacy

will inspire those around you—especially your children.

Conclusion

Rewriting your story is not only a profound responsibility but also an extraordinary gift that can transcend the boundaries of your own life and significantly impact the lives of those connected to you.

As you embark on this transformative journey, consider the immense influence you have in shaping the patterns and narratives that will be passed down through generations. By consciously choosing to declare generational blessings, you set in motion a powerful legacy that resonates far beyond your immediate family or community.

Every small shift you make in your perspective or actions can create ripples, extending outward and affecting those around you in ways you may not fully comprehend. These changes can inspire others, foster healing in relationships, and uplift spirits—creating a network of positivity that nurtures and encourages future generations. Your story is a rich tapestry woven from experiences, lessons, and moments of triumph and vulnerability, and it holds the potential to inspire countless others.

When you embrace the chance to craft a narrative that echoes through time, think of the impact it can have. This legacy can become a source of strength and guidance for those who come after you, reflecting themes of love, resilience, courage, and an unwavering belief in the possibility of a brighter, more hopeful future. Your narrative can serve as a beacon of light, illustrating the beauty of perseverance and the importance of remaining steadfast in the face of challenges. In this way, your story becomes not just an account of your life but a cherished inheritance—more valuable than any material possession—rich with wisdom and insight that can uplift and empower generations to come.

CHAPTER 7

Cultivating a Mindset of Abundance

Shifting from Scarcity to Abundance

As we journey through life, our perceptions shape the experiences we encounter.

One of the most transformative shifts we can make is moving from a mindset of scarcity to a mindset of abundance. This chapter will explore how this shift not only changes our perception but also profoundly impacts our actions, relationships, and overall well-being.

Understanding Scarcity vs. Abundance

Scarcity is rooted in fear and the belief that resources, opportunities, and love are limited. When we operate from a scarcity mindset, we tend to hoard what we have, whether it be money, time, or generosity. This fear can lead to anxiety, comparison with others, and a cycle of dissatisfaction.

Conversely, an abundance mindset embraces the belief that there is more than enough for everyone. It recognizes that opportunities are plentiful, resources are available, and the universe is ever-expanding. Adopting this perspective allows us to share freely, take calculated risks, and approach life with confidence and hope.

The Transformation Process

1. **Awareness**: The first step to shifting from scarcity to abundance is awareness. Begin to notice your thoughts and feelings surrounding money,

relationships, and opportunities. Are they rooted in fear or belief?

2. **Challenge Negative Beliefs**: Once you recognize scarcity-based thoughts, challenge them. Are they true? Is this belief serving you or hindering your growth?

3. **Cultivate Gratitude**: Abundance flourishes in the soil of gratitude. Make it a daily practice to list three things you are grateful for. This simple act helps shift your focus from what is lacking to what is present and valuable in your life.

4. **Set Abundant Goals**: Instead of limiting yourself with small, cautious objectives, set goals that inspire you and open the door to new possibilities. Create an action plan that aligns with an abundance mindset.

5. **Surround Yourself with Abundance**: Engage with people who embody an abundance mindset. Their energy will uplift you and encourage you to see the possibilities around you.

Scriptural Insights

The wisdom found in scripture offers profound guidance on

cultivating an abundance mindset. Here are several key verses that can inspire and reinforce this perspective:

Philippians 4:19 (NIV)

"And my God will meet all your needs according to the riches of his glory in Christ Jesus."

This verse reassures us that we are provided for beyond our immediate understanding. Trusting that our needs are met opens us to the fullness of life.

2 Corinthians 9:8 (NIV)

"And God is able to bless you abundantly, so that in all things at all times, having all that you need, you will abound in every good work." This scripture highlights the cyclical nature of abundance. As we receive and recognize God's blessings, we are equipped to give and uplift others.

Matthew 6:33 (NIV)

"But seek first his kingdom and his righteousness, and all these things will be given to you as well."

When we focus on what truly matters—our purpose and relationship with the Divine—everything else aligns, and our lives become filled with abundance.

Daily Affirmations for Abundance

Affirmations serve as powerful tools to reinforce our mindset. Here are some daily affirmations to support your shift towards abundance:

1. I am worthy of abundance in all areas of my life.
2. I release all fears around scarcity and embrace the flow of prosperity.
3. Opportunities are drawn to me, and I am open to receiving them.

4. I am grateful for the abundance that surrounds me every day.
5. I contribute my talents and gifts freely, knowing that there is plenty to go around.
6. I trust in the process of life and my ability to manifest my dreams.

7. **I celebrate the success of others, knowing it does not diminish my own potential.**

Integrating These Principles into Daily Life

To truly cultivate a mindset of abundance, it's essential to integrate these insights and practices into your everyday life. Start by committing to a daily routine that includes reflection, gratitude, and affirmations. Surround yourself with books, podcasts, and communities that reinforce an abundance mentality.

In moments of doubt or fear, revisit the scripture and affirmations. Allow them to serve as anchors that ground you in the truth of abundance. Remember, the more you practice this shift in perspective, the more natural it will become.

Conclusion

Cultivating a mindset of abundance is not something that happens overnight; rather, it is a gradual process that involves continuous growth and transformation. This journey requires patience and persistence, as it often challenges deep-seated beliefs shaped by experiences of scarcity. By actively working to shift your perspective from one of lack to one of abundance, you will not only enrich your own life but also create a ripple effect that positively influences those around you.

As you embark on this transformative path, take the time to recognize the various forms of abundance that exist in your life—be it love, health, creativity, or financial resources. Each of these elements can flourish when nurtured with intention and gratitude. Embrace this journey wholeheartedly, and you may find that abundance begins to flow into your life in unexpected and delightful ways, manifesting as new opportunities, deeper relationships, or increased creativity.

As we come to the end of this chapter, I invite you to pause and reflect on your unique journey. What specific desires do you wish to cultivate more of in your life? Consider the areas where you seek growth and fulfillment. Remember, the seeds of abundance are already within you—waiting to be nurtured. By dedicating time and energy to these aspirations, allowing room for them to develop and flourish, you'll create a life rich with possibilities and joy.

CHAPTER 8

The Importance of Community

In a world where individualism is often celebrated, the power of community is a profound and transformative force that can't be overlooked. We thrive not just on our skills and talents, but also on the connections we foster with others. In this chapter, we will explore the significance of building support systems, the invaluable role of mentorship, and the need for accountability within communities.

Building Support Systems

The concept of a support system can take many forms—

be it family, friends, co-workers, or even acquaintances who share similar interests or goals. A support system acts as a safety net, providing encouragement, advice, and companionship during both the peaks and valleys of life's journey.

The Pillars of Support

1. **Emotional Support**: Often, the greatest gift we can offer each other is a listening ear. Whether through informal gatherings or structured meet-ups, emotional support allows individuals to share their experiences, fears, and aspirations. This communal sharing

fosters resilience, nurturing individuals who might otherwise feel isolated in their struggles.

2. **Practical Support**: Communities can also rally together to provide practical help. Whether it's organizing a meal train for a family in

need, pooling resources to assist someone in financial distress, or collaborating on projects, practical support enhances the quality of life and builds a sense of belonging.

3. **Information Sharing**: In this digital age,

communities can disseminate information rapidly. Whether it is social media groups or local meet-ups centered around specific interests, sharing knowledge and expertise is essential. These networks allow individuals to stay informed about opportunities, emerging issues, and resources that can aid their personal and professional growth.

Building Your Community

Creating a robust support system begins with intention. Start by identifying the areas in your life where you seek support and then actively seek out communities that align with those needs. Whether it's a local hobby group, a professional organization, or an advocacy community, getting involved is the first step.

Be Proactive: Attend events, volunteer, join online forums, and don't hesitate to reach out to others. Building a community requires effort but is incredibly rewarding. Remember that communities thrive on reciprocity. The more you contribute, the more you'll gain.

The Role of Mentorship

Mentorship serves as one of the cornerstones of a supportive community. A mentor acts as a guide, offering wisdom, experience, and perspective that can be transformative for the mentee.

The Benefits of Mentorship

1. **Guided Learning**: Mentors share invaluable insights, helping mentees navigate challenges more effectively. This

relationship allows for tailored advice that can accelerate learning and development.

2. **Networking Opportunities**: A mentor often has access to a vast network of contacts that can introduce mentees to opportunities, helping

them to expand their horizons in ways they might not have envisioned.

3. **Accountability**: Mentors hold mentees accountable for their goals. This sense of responsibility can drive progress, as having someone invested in

your growth encourages you to remain committed.

Becoming a Mentor

While seeking mentorship is vital, giving back to the community by becoming a mentor is equally important. Share your experiences, listen actively, and provide guidance to those who are seeking to learn. The cyclical nature of mentorship fosters a culture of growth and success, as knowledge is passed down and cultivated.

The Need for Accountability

Accountability within a community can serve as a powerful motivator. When individuals commit to their goals and share them with others, they are more likely to follow through.

Creating an Accountability Framework

1. **Goal-Setting Groups**: Form or join groups where members set specific, measurable goals and meet regularly to share their progress. This not only fosters a

sense of accountability but also allows for collaboration and sharing of strategies.

2. **Peer Check-Ins**: Nurturing accountability doesn't require formal structures—a simple system of checking in with a peer can work wonders. This can be as

simple as a text or a quick coffee chat where progress is discussed and celebrated.

3. **Celebrate Small Wins**: In a world that sometimes focuses too heavily on grand achievements, recognizing and celebrating small

victories within a community fosters an environment of encouragement and positivity. It reminds individuals that every step forward is part of a larger journey toward success.

Conclusion

The significance of community in the establishment of robust support systems is profound and cannot be emphasized enough. Communities serve as a vital backbone for individuals, offering a network of relationships that foster both personal and collective growth. By nurturing connections among members and engaging in mentorship programs, individuals can access a wealth of knowledge and experiences. This shared journey creates opportunities for accountability, motivating each person to strive for their goals while providing encouragement to others in the group.

As we navigate the complexities of life, the idea of embarking on this journey alone can often feel daunting.

However, with a supportive community, life's challenges are transformed into a shared adventure, enriched by the diverse contributions and perspectives of each member. The exchange of ideas, emotional support, and practical assistance fosters an environment where everyone can flourish.

Whether you're in need of support or in a position to offer it, recognizing and embracing the importance of community is a truly transformative experience. It cultivates a sense of belonging and enhances the overall quality of life, leading to deeper connections and a more fulfilling existence. In unity, we discover not only strength but also the potential to thrive in ways we couldn't imagine alone. Together, we are stronger, and together, we can achieve remarkable things.

THE END

A Journey of Hope and Transformation

As we draw near to the end of our journey, it is essential to take a moment to reflect on the profound changes we have undergone, as well as the multitude of blessings that still lie ahead. Throughout this journey, we have uncovered invaluable insights and have been reminded of the transformative power of faith. In this reflective space, we encourage our readers to continually nurture and deepen their relationship with God. This connection serves not only as a source of strength and guidance but also as a wellspring from which blessings overflow.

As we receive the grace of these blessings, we are called to share them generously with the lives of others around us. This leads to the creation of a lasting legacy—one built on the principles of faith, hope, and love. By extending these blessings, we can uplift those in need, inspire change in our communities, and cultivate an environment where hope can flourish.

Appendix: Resources for Further Study

To support my readers on this transformative journey, an extensive list of resources will be provided. This includes carefully selected books that delve deeper into themes of faith, personal growth, and spiritual transformation. I will also compile relevant scriptures that can offer solace and guidance during challenging times. Additionally, l will highlight various online resources—such as courses, podcasts, and webinars—that can further enrich your understanding and experience.

Finally, I will introduce communities and support groups where individuals can connect with others on a similar path. These opportunities for fellowship can foster discussion, encouragement, and shared wisdom, making the journey not just an individual experience but a collective one as well. Together, let us continue this journey of hope and transformation, knowing that through our efforts, we can create a ripple effect of positive change in the world around us.

Lists of Bible Verses to Meditate to Help You Breaking Generational Curses

Exodus 20:5 - Thou shalt not bow down thyself to them, nor serve them: for I the LORD thy God am a jealous God, visiting the iniquity of the fathers upon the children unto the third and fourth generation of them that hate me;

Deuteronomy 28:1-68 - And it shall come to pass, if thou shalt hearken diligently unto the voice of the LORD thy God, to observe and to do all his commandments which I command thee this day, that the LORD thy God will set thee on high above all nations of the earth: *(Read More...)*

Jeremiah 17:5 - Thus saith the LORD; Cursed be the man that trusteth in man, and maketh flesh his arm, and whose heart departeth from the LORD.

Galatians 3:13 - Christ hath redeemed us from the curse of the law, being made a curse for us: for it is written, Cursed is every one that hangeth on a tree:

Ephesians 6:12 - For we wrestle not against flesh and blood, but against principalities, against powers, against the rulers of the darkness of this world, against spiritual wickedness in high places.

Ezekiel 18:19-20 - Yet say ye, Why? doth not the son bear the iniquity of the father? When the son hath done that which is lawful and right, and hath kept all my statutes, and hath done them, he shall surely live. (*Read More…*)

James 5:16 - Confess your faults one to another, and pray one for another, that ye may be healed. The effectual fervent prayer of a righteous man availeth much.

Romans 8:2 - For the law of the Spirit of life in Christ Jesus hath made me free from the law of sin and death.

1 John 1:9 - If we confess our sins, he is faithful and just to forgive us our sins, and to cleanse us from all unrighteousness.

Proverbs 18:21 - Death and life are in the power of the tongue: and they that love it shall eat the fruit thereof.

Psalms 103:1-22 - (A Psalm of David.) Bless the LORD, O my soul: and all that is within me, bless his holy name. *(Read More...)*

Numbers 14:18 - The LORD is longsuffering, and of great mercy, forgiving iniquity and transgression, and by no means clearing the guilty, visiting the iniquity of the fathers upon the children unto the third and fourth generation.

Matthew 16:19 - And I will give unto thee the keys of the kingdom of heaven: and whatsoever thou shalt bind on earth shall be bound in heaven: and whatsoever thou shalt loose on earth shall be loosed in heaven.

Galatians 3:13-14 - Christ hath redeemed us from the curse of the law, being made a curse for us: for it is written, Cursed is every one that hangeth on a tree: *(Read More....)*

Genesis 12:3 - And I will bless them that bless thee, and curse him that curseth thee: and in thee shall all families of the earth be blessed.

Proverbs 26:2 - As the bird by wandering, as the swallow by flying, so the curse causeless shall not come.

Isaiah 54:17 - No weapon that is formed against thee shall prosper; and every tongue that shall rise against thee in judgment thou shalt condemn. This is the heritage of the servants of the LORD, and their righteousness is of me, saith the LORD.

Deuteronomy 5:9 - Thou shalt not bow down thyself unto them, nor serve them: for I the LORD thy God am a jealous God, visiting the iniquity of the fathers upon the children unto the third and fourth generation of them that hate me,

2 Corinthians 5:17 - Therefore if any man be in Christ, he is a new creature: old things are passed away; behold, all things are become new.

ACKNOWLEDGMENT

A sincere and heartfelt appreciation will be extended to all those who played a pivotal role in bringing this book to fruition. Their unwavering support and contributions have been invaluable in this creative journey. In addition, readers are encouraged to actively engage in ongoing dialogue, not only with God but also with one another, to foster a sense of community and shared growth.

"Breaking the Chains" is designed to be a transformative guide, intricately weaving together the threads of personal stories, spiritual insights, and practical strategies. Its purpose is to lead individuals away from the burdens of their painful histories and towards a future brimming with hope, healing, and generational blessings. This journey of transformation is rooted in the principles of faith and community.

Readers will discover actionable insights that empower them to make meaningful changes in their lives. More importantly, they will find the strength to alter the narratives of their families for generations to come. By embracing this guide, individuals can break free from cycles of despair and cultivate a legacy filled with resilience, love, and positive impact.

ABOUT THE AUTHOR

At the age of 25, she took a bold step into the literary world by publishing her debut book, "Amid My Questionable Existence." This poignant work delves deeply into the intricacies of personal challenges, exploring the tumultuous journey of self-discovery amid both internal conflicts and external obstacles. Through her writing, Rachel invites readers to reflect on their struggles and triumphs, providing a relatable perspective that resonates widely.

Following the success of her first book, Rachel went on to author several additional publications, each infused with the wisdom and insights she has gathered throughout her life. Her books serve not only as a source of inspiration but also as a guide for navigating the complexities of modern existence.

With humble beginnings that shaped her character and aspirations, Rachel developed an undeniable passion for music early in her life. She draws upon a rich tapestry of influences to craft her unique sound, which fuses modern and orchestral elements with contemporary themes. Her music transcends generational divides, offering a refreshing blend of hope and positivity that encourages listeners to envision a brighter future.

Through her art, Rachel Tugutu continues to inspire and uplift, leaving a lasting impact on those who encounter her work.

TO GOD BE THE GLORY!!!

www.ingramcontent.com/pod-product-compliance
Lightning Source LLC
LaVergne TN
LVHW011933070526
838202LV00054B/4618